D1587873

# COLORADO
## For The First Time

PHOTOGRAPHY BY CLAUDE STEELMAN

WESTERN REFLECTIONS
PUBLISHING COMPANY

*To my mother, Faye Steelman. For all the years of love, support, and encouragement.*

© Claude Steelman
All rights reserved including the right of reproduction in whole or in part

Any commercial use of this book by dismantling and selling prints framed or unframed, or using any part for any form of reproduction is strictly prohibited.

First Printing 2005
Printed in China
Library of Congress Catalog Card No. 2004101745

ISBN-13: 978-1-890437-96-1
ISBN-10: 1-890437-96-4

Jacket design, book design, typography:
SJS Design, (Susan Smilanic) and Laurie Goralka Design
Cover photo: Elk at Long's Peak

Introduction by P. David Smith

First Edition

Claude Steelman
WildShots
www.wildshots.com

Western Reflections Publishing Co.®
219 Main Street
Montrose, Colorado 81401
U.S.A.
www.westernreflectionspub.com

DEAD HORSE CREEK

As I write I am only twenty-five miles from them [Rocky Mountains], and they are gradually gaining possession of me. I can look at and feel nothing else.

Isabella Lucy Bird, 1800s, Greeley

*A Lady's Life in the Rocky Mountains*

MOUNTAIN BLUEBIRDS

Hanging Lake

MULE DEER FAWN

ASPEN AND EVERGREENS

HUMMINGBIRD ON A CONE FLOWER

PAWNEE BUTTES

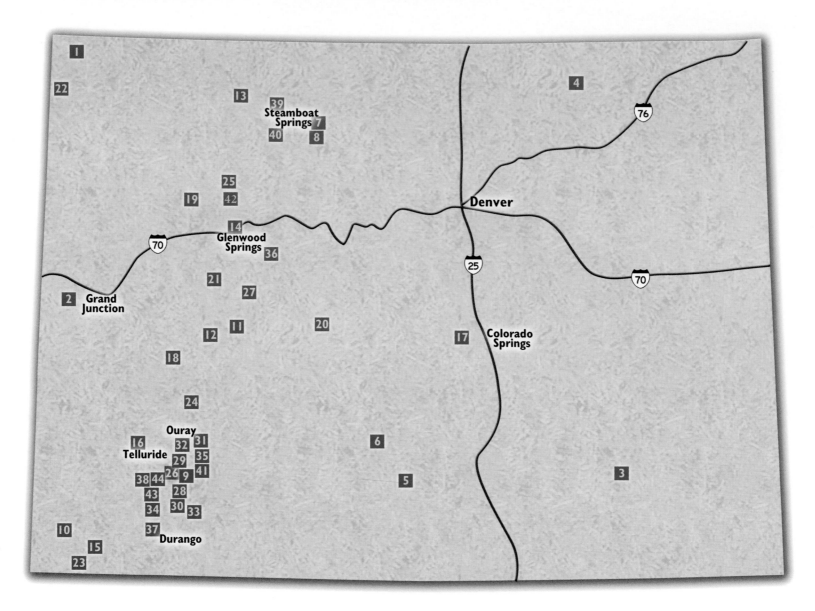

American Basin

# INTRODUCTION

Seeing Colorado for the first time is an experience that many will never forget, from the first courageous pioneers in search of a better life to the present-day traveler wanting to capture a glimpse of the beauty they have only heard or read about in the travel brochures. For those who have resided in Colorado for several years, they may begin to take their surroundings for granted and need to be reminded and encouraged to take the time and effort to once again look – to really look – at this awesome land. This renewed vision can help longtime residents to realize just how intertwined they are with the land and water, the wildlife, and the vegetation of Colorado. For the first time they may begin to notice the little flowers in the tundra, the beauty of a ptarmigan in the snow, or even the infinite designs of snowflakes.

Anyone who has entered Colorado has been greatly impacted, beginning with the Paleo Indians who moved into what would become Colorado 6,000 years ago. It certainly continued with the Ute Indians who lived in harmony with what they called "the Shining Mountains" for over 500 years. Colorado captured the hearts of the rugged trappers who searched its sparkling clean rivers for beaver and the prospectors who crawled all over its indomitable peaks searching for gold and silver. The first settlers developed a deep respect for this region when forced to deal with the harsh weather conditions and the fortress of mountains that seemed to block their way. It awed and inspired the ranchers and farmers who settled on its seemingly endless plains, and the splendor of Colorado eventually inspired Katharine Lee Bates to write "America The Beautiful" from the top of Pike's Peak.

Colorado continues to contain a spirit that captures the heart of all who come. It is a land that inspires, uplifts, and gratifies all who visit, work, or are lucky enough to live here. The environment hones and sharpens the senses of its inhabitants like fine steel sharpens a good knife. The magnificent and rugged land attracts and forms impressive and independent people who love and are inspired by its awesome grandeur. It is a home for the heart and soul.

The true essence of what draws people to Colorado, and always seems to bring them back, at least in their hearts, is difficult to grasp, but Claude Steelman has tried to do just that by capturing the mysteries, the moments, and the magic of Colorado and its natural inhabitants in this stunning book of photographs. Through his works of art, Claude explains the magnetism of the state that is so hard to put into words, but which many, from the early pioneers to present-day travelers, have tried to do. We have included some of the quotes, past and present, of those experiencing Colorado for the first time.

My own story is just one of the over three million stories of the inhabitants of Colorado and the millions of visitors seeing the state for the first time. They are all different, yet they all have their similarities. The first time that I saw Colorado was not a particular moment in time, but rather the entire summer of 1949. I was five years old and my grandparents drove into our driveway in Dallas, Texas, before daylight. It was the Saturday of Memorial Day weekend, and we drove hard all that day and still didn't make it to Colorado by dark. I don't remember what Colorado looked like the first time I physically saw it the next day, but I do remember the smell of the cool, crisp air that first summer morning and how different it was from the hot, humid air of Texas.

It still took the entire daylight hours of that second day to finally make it to our destination, which was my grandparents' new summer cabin that had been built by unemployed Crested Butte coal miners on Spring Creek, a tributary of the Taylor River. I spent the next wondrous 100 days there – not returning to Texas until Labor Day weekend.

Rattlesnake in Prickly Pear Cactus

Although my life experience was certainly limited at the ripe old age of five, it was an entirely different world than what I was used to in Texas. The precipitous mountains were certainly overwhelming and inspiring, but it was the little things that I remember. The sound and smell of crackling fires of aspen in the open fireplace in the early evening of a summer day! The sight of rocks the size of automobiles to climb and play games on. Chipmunk traps made from wood boxes and screens brought us an up close look at a little creature I had never seen before, and fishing for the first time in the clear mountain streams.

The next year I again came to Colorado for the entire summer and continued to learn the intricacies of fly fishing. I walked through high mountain meadows, drank out of the clear mountain streams (not a practice that I would advise today), and donned my raincoat or hid under a tree to wait out a sudden mountain shower. I was usually by myself when fishing, although there was always an adult somewhere ahead and behind me in the river. I saw mule deer and elk for the first time and spent time watching the birds swooping after the bugs along the creek.

The next summer my grandfather suffered a severe stroke. I went to Colorado, but this time to a boys' summer camp – Ute Trail Ranch near Lake City. It was absolute heaven for a small boy of eight, but it was to be my last trip to paradise for some time. I was only to see Colorado in my dreams for the next fifteen years.

After I graduated from law school, I made a short visit to Colorado and was able to experience the state for the first time from an RV. It was marvelous to spend the night beside a small mountain stream and to eat lunch while watching deer grazing in the nearby meadows. That trip convinced me that my family and I must find some way to live in this awe-inspiring state.

We eventually began to make several trips each year to Colorado, which included at least one winter trip for our newly discovered sport – skiing. Colorado in the winter was a whole new world. The stillness of snow falling, the clouds wrapping around the mountains, and the deer and elk, which were so approachable during winter, were all exciting new sights for a Texas family.

On the 4th of July of the bicentennial year we moved to Colorado. Then there were all kinds of firsts. The first snow we experienced in June. The first time we almost stepped on a young motionless fawn while hiking through the woods. The first time I experienced the power of an avalanche or felt the excitement of a summer thunderstorm high in the mountains. There was the first time I stopped to really look up close at the high mountain tundra in the summer or the flock of ptarmigan that I actually nudged with my feet, as they were so well hidden. Then there was the first time that I sat with my children at the top of a Colorado Fourteener, looking out at an endless supply of mountains and realized just how small I really am in this world. Or the time I lay with a close friend in a flowery mountain meadow, watching the slowly forming clouds and a herd of bighorn sheep grazing nearby.

Yes, there are a lot of first times in Colorado – each a new and exciting experience that binds us more closely to our state. They are occasions when we will come to better know the simpler but more meaningful things of life – nature, beauty, and the lives of our natural inhabitants. And I know for myself that there will be many more "first times" for me, and I look forward to them every time I venture into the great outdoors of Colorado.

As you begin your journey through this book, take the time to study each photograph so that you do not miss the snake tucked in next to the cactus, the curious pica viewing her domain from the safety of her fortress of rocks, or the bear cub nestled against its mother.

Also, take notice of what senses are stirred when viewing these photographs, such as a sense of wonder, awe, longing, well-being, reverence, inspiration, comfort, peace, solitude, passion, respect, mystery, intelligence, integrity, harmony, and joy. Maybe then you can begin to articulate for yourself what you felt the first time you saw Colorado.

P. David Smith
Publisher/Author

Frozen Waterfall

False Hellebore and Larkspur

Raccoon

ANIMAS RIVER

BALD EAGLE

ASPEN IN SNOW, ROUTT COUNTY

SNOWSHOE HARE

SQUIRRELTAIL GRASS

Mallards

LA PLATA CANYON

AMERICAN AVOCET

The first time I saw Colorado it was a classic case of love at first sight. It was the early seventies and I had come from Florida to work as a wrangler on a dude ranch in the Winter Park area. I immediately fell in love with the mountains. It was so different from where I had grown up — the big vistas, the clear mountain streams, the spectacular wildflower blooms, and the abundant wildlife. All of my spare time was spent in the outdoors seeing as much of Colorado's natural beauty as possible. Though I have been here for thirty years. I am still seeing Colorado for the first time. With a state so diverse, there will always be new places to see, explore, and capture on film.

Claude Steelman, 1970s, Winter Park
Photographer

It was thick with willows, bush-maples, and alders. Then branches brushed into our faces, they grew so close: flowers burst into our sight like magic on all sides. — fireweed, harebells, painter's-brush, larkspur, asters of all colors and superbly full and large. It was a fairy garden. The grass was green. — real, perfect green grass, the first, the only true green grass I have ever seen in Colorado. Except for the towering and stony walls above our head and for the fiery scarlet of the painter's brush and the tall spikes of larkspur. I could have fancied myself in a wild thicketed cave in Vermont.

Helen Hunt Jackson, 1870s, near South Park
*Westward to a High Mountain*

Rifle Falls

Claret Cup Cactus

Badger

Paintbrush and Mountain Stream

MUDDY PASS LAKE

ENGINE CREEK WATERFALL

FEMALE MALLARD

MOUNTAIN BLUEBIRD

Wildflowers, Comanche National Grassland

No greater diversity of natural resources did the Almighty ever plant in an equal area.... Perennial streams, as pure as crystal, come down from eternal snowbanks....

Alfred Castner King, 1890s
*Mountain Idylls and Other Poems*

PARRY'S PRIMROSE

BEAVER

WHITE PELICANS

CHIMING BELLS

STONEY PASS

MARMOT

YANKEE BOY BASIN/TWIN
FALLS

BROADTAIL HUMMINGBIRD
WITH YOUNG

YANKEE BOY BASIN

SUNRISE, COMANCHE NATIONAL GRASSLAND

WILD ROSE AND ASPEN

RED PAINTBRUSH

COLUMBINE AND ASPEN

WHITE RIVER NATIONAL FOREST

RUFOUS HUMMINGBIRD

BLUE GROUSE

Wood Duck

Common Chicory

Their [plains] surface is covered with close, low grasses, — amber-brown, golden yellow, and claret red in winter, in summer of a pale olive green, far less beautiful, vivid, and vitalized than the browns and yellows and reds of the winter. But in the summer come myriads of flowers, lighting up the olive green background, making it into a mosaic of white and purple and pink and scarlet and scarlet and yellow.

Helen Hunt Jackson, 1870s, Colorado Springs
*Westward to a High Mountain*

. . . I had begun to like this land and its ways. I felt close to its animals and birds and sparse growing things, its silence, even its loneliness. Its loneliness stretched my soul beyond my years to a mysterious sense of a time when I should reach that far land's end and lift up the sky to enter the lives and the worlds I had no need to know until then.

Sonora Babb, 1913, plains of Colorado
*An Owl on Every Post*

LYNX PASS

PAWNEE NATIONAL GRASSLAND

SNEFFELS RANGE SUNRISE

'We turned around and around to see the full circle of horizon, the perfect meeting of earth and sky.... 'We were at once in a grand and endless space, and enclosed, locked in.

Sanora Babb, 1913
*An Owl on Every Post*

SUNRISE, FLAT TOPS WILDERNESS

Lily Pond, San Juan National Forest

Wildflowers near Coffee Pot Spring

RED MOUNTAIN PASS

DALLAS DIVIDE

Wildflowers in Fog, Muddy Pass

Mountain Goat

SANDHILL CRANE

SUNSET, MOLAS PASS

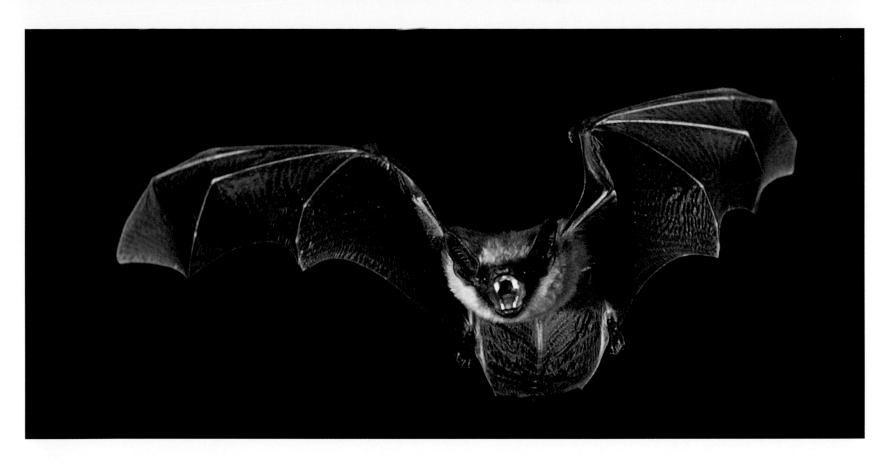

MYOTIS BAT

SUNRISE, PAWNEE NATIONAL GRASSLAND

Oak Brush Sunset, Mesa Verde National Park

SUNRISE AT MEDANO CREEK

APPROACHING STORM, ROUTT COUNTY

PAWNEE BUTTES

there is no way I'm going to keep quiet about it. It was chock full of surprises. I don't know how I thought the color change would happen, but I was surprised at the aspen's gradual paling to a lighter green. Such a subtle prelude marked by an occasional startling dash of yellow. I had been told that aspen groves would look like honey flowing down the mountain. They didn't tell me about the breathtaking strands of red and variegated orange. Who would have thought that the common cottonwood would join in the act? I was not prepared for the medley of ground foliage - yellow, red, forming graceful patterns on slopes and bluffs.

The aspen far up the rugged heights, "confessing the gentlest breeze," was just changing into the sere and yellow leaf of the dying year. The sides of the mountain, clothed in the purple hues of scrubby oak leaf and flora, indigenous to the state of Colorado, and adorned with a bouquet here and there of pine or spruce, offered a delightful picture to the lover of the wild and romantic in nature.

Rev. J. J. Gibbons, 1890, Ophir Range
*In the San Juan*

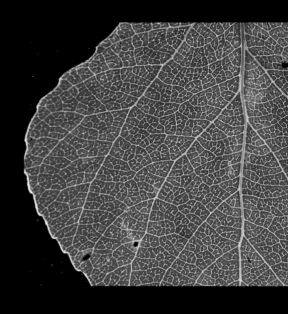

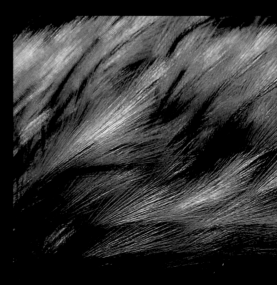

ASPEN LEAF

WESTERN GREBE

SQUIRRELTAIL GRASS

THREE-LEAF SUMAC, ANIMAS RIVER

Red Fox Kit

WILD GERANIUM AND MEADOWRUE

ASPEN LEAVES

SNEFFELS RANGE

'When I first saw California Gulch. I knew that I had finally found my spiritual center. I relive that feeling every time I visit the site. The colors of the mountain blend with the muted hues of the plants and old wood to create a sublime canvas no artist could paint.

Carol McManus, 1978
*author*

BIGHORN SHEEP

DALLAS DIVIDE

Aspen and Mountain Ash

LA PLATA RIVER

GREAT HORNED OWL

GUNNISON NATIONAL FOREST

CRYSTAL LAKE AND RED MOUNTAINS

MOUNTAIN ASH, RABBIT EARS PASS                    COTTONWOOD TREES ALONG LA PLATA RIVER

MAROON BELLS

WHITE RIVER NATIONAL FOREST

MULE DEER

SAGE GROUSE STRUTTING

Chalk Creek Falls

Rainbow Trout

KEBLER PASS

FALL ASPEN

Fifteen miles more over great ridges, along passes dark with shadow, and so narrow that we had to ride in the beds of the streams which had excavated them round the bases of colossal pyramids of rock crested with pines, up into fair upland "parks," scarlet in patches with the poison oak, parks so beautifully arranged by nature that I momentarily expected to come upon some stately mansion, but that afternoon crested blue jays and chipmunks had them all to themselves. Here, in the early morning, deer, bighorn, and the stately elk, come down to feed, and there, in the night, prowl and growl the Rocky Mountain lion, the grizzly bear, and the cowardly wolf.

Isabella Lucy Bird, 1800s, St. Vrain Canyon
*A Lady's Life in the Rocky Mountains*

PRIMROSE

McElmo Canyon

Red Fox

COLORADO RIVER, GLENWOOD CANYON

GREAT HORNED OWL

Baneberry in Bracken Fern

BROADTAIL HUMMINGBIRD ON COLUMBINE

MILK SNAKE

MOREL MUSHROOM

As I looked down upon those fiery flaming mountains which no painter's brush could exaggerate, and off to the sharp peaks and ranges beyond, rising tier above tier until the most distant ones seemed to support the horizon, my soul was filled to overflowing with the joy of magnificent mountain scenery.

Roselle Theodore Cross, late 1800s, Red Mountain
*My Mountains*

MOUNTAIN GOAT

COLORADO NATIONAL MONUMENT

DINOSAUR TRACKS, PICKETWIRE CANYON

Balanced Rock, Colorado National Monument

Sandstone Arch, Rattlesnake Canyon

KISSING CAMELS, GARDEN OF THE GODS

GARDEN OF THE GODS

Sandstone Formation, Sand Canyon

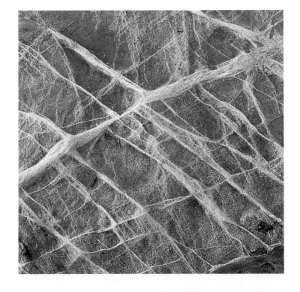

PURGATOIRE RIVER

DINOSAUR NATIONAL MONUMENT

GATES OF LODORE

Six miles of drab plain were relieved only by the cactus blossoms. These were abundant and beautiful, chiefly of the prickly pear variety, great mats of uncouth, bristling leaves, looking like oblong, green griddle-cakes, made thick and stuck full of pins, points out, — as repellant a plant as is to be found anywhere on the face of the earth; but lo! out of the edge of this thick and unseemly lobe springs a many-leaved chalice of satin sheen, graceful, nay, regal in its poise, in its quiet. No breeze stirs it; no sun wilts it; no other blossom rivals the lustrous transparency of its petals. Of all shades of yellow, from the pales cream-color up to the deepest tint of virgin gold; of all shades of pink, form a faint, hardly perceptible flush, up to a rose as clear and bright as that in the palm of a baby's hand. Myriads of these, full-blown, half-blown, and in bud, we saw on every rod of the six miles of desolate drab plains which we crossed below Canyon City.

Helen Hunt Jackson, 1878, near Canyon City
*Westward to a High Mountain*

They apparently drew near to me, as though they would mutely welcome a new lover, and as they began to surround and close in on me there came over me a sense of their beauty and grandeur that almost overwhelmed me, and made me feel that I must go back at once and get my wife to come and enjoy with me that new and delightful sensation. It was a clear case of love at first sight, for it was my first sight of mountains close at hand. I did not realize what glorious times I was to have with them in the years to come. As I turned towards home I left with them an unspoken appointment to call on them again and to call often.

Roselle Theodore Cross, 1876, Manitou Springs
*My Mountains*

CRINOID FOSSILS

ORB SPIDER

GREAT SAND DUNES
NATIONAL PARK AND PRESERVE

MEDANO CREEK, SAND DUNES

Prairie Falcon Chicks

PRICKLY PEAR CACTUS

Claret Cup Cactus

CHIMNEY ROCK

PAINTBRUSH AND SANDSTONE

CACTUS AND SANDSTONE, SAND CANYON

CACTUS                                          COMANCHE NATIONAL GRASSLAND

It gave me a strange sensation to embark upon the Plains. Plains everywhere. plains generally level. elsewhere rolling in long undulations. like the waves of a sea which had fallen asleep.

Isabella Lucy Bird, 1800s, Fort Collins
*A Lady's Life in the Rocky Mountains*

GREAT SAND DUNES NATIONAL PARK AND PRESERVE

Praying Mantis

COLLARED LIZARD

BISON, SAN LUIS VALLEY

ABRAMS MOUNTAIN

ABERT'S SQUIRREL

"Never, nowhere, have I seen anything to equal the view into Estes Park. The mountains "of the land which is very far off" are very near now, but the near is more glorious than the far, and reality than dreamland. The mountain fever seized me, and, giving my tireless horse one encouraging word, he dashed at full gallop over a mile of smooth sward at delirious speed.

Isabella Lucy Bird, 1800s, Estes Park
*A Lady's Life in the Rocky Mountains*

"Coming home to a place he'd never been before." A quote from one of John Denver's songs explains exactly how I felt when I first entered Colorado in 1988. There was an immediate instinctual connection, a guttural feeling that this was the place where I most wanted to be. I felt in complete harmony with the unbelievable beauty that surrounded me and a sense of peace enveloped my whole being. The glorious mountains were symbols of strength and endurance as I settled into my new surroundings and the endless skies opened my heart to dream all kinds of possibilities. My home now truly is in Colorado.

Carole London, 1988, eastern Colorado

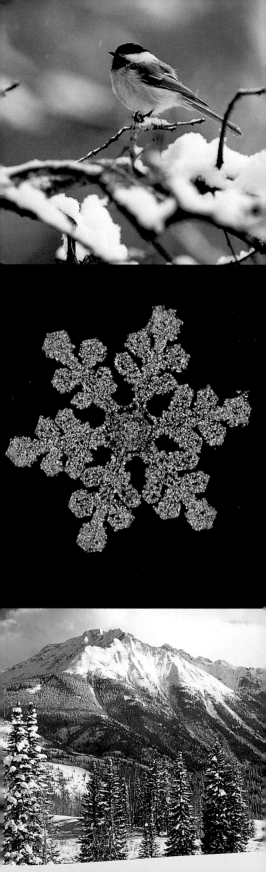

PINON PINE

CASCADE CREEK

FROZEN WATERFALL, OURAY

UNCOMPAHGRE NATIONAL FOREST

ELK

MOUNTAIN LION

FLORIDA RIVER

ASPEN IN SNOW

SNOW ON OAK BRUSH

There was no sound, no sight, no trace of human life. The silence, the sense of space in these Rocky Mountains solitudes cannot be expressed; neither can the peculiar atmospheric beauty be described. It is the result partly of the great distances, partly of the rarefied air.

Helen Hunt Jackson, 1874
*Westward to a High Mountain*

San Juan National Forest

BLACK BEAR AND CUB, ROCKY MOUNTAIN NATIONAL PARK

BIGHORN SHEEP

San Juan National Forest

Coal Bank Pass

Molas Lake

RED MOUNTAIN PASS

PTARMIGAN

ASPEN AND WINTER SUN

RIFLE FALLS

SANDSTONE, SAND CANYON

WESTERN TANAGER

# TECHNICAL DATA

I shot all the photographs for this book on transparency film with a 35mm camera system. The camera bodies were the Nikon FE2, F3, F4, and N90. I used a variety of Nikon lenses from 24mm to 500mm, the 24mm being my primary landscape lens and the 500mm being the primary wildlife lens.

As for film, I used Fujichrome Velvia ASA 50 for most of the scenic and macro shots and Fujichrome Provia ASA 100 for the wildlife photographs. These fine-grained films make excellent prints and also reproduce extremely well with the four-color printing process that was used in this book.

For the high speed photographs of the hummingbirds and bats in flight, I used a four flash setup with Metz flashes set to fire at 14000th of a second in order to stop the action. Underwater photographs were taken with a Nikon N90 and 24mm lens housed in an Ikelite underwater housing. The extreme close-up photographs, such as the snowflakes, were captured using an Olympus system with bellows and a ring flash.

Last but not least are the tripods. I used a Gitzo 410 for the bigger lenses and a Bogen 3021 for the mid-range and wide-angle lenses. If I could give only one photography tip to a beginning photographer, it would be to use a tripod whenever possible. It not only makes for sharper images, it is a great aid in composing a photograph.